THE RED CORAL HOUSE

Written by Jeff Hartman
Illustrated by Kate Horton

This book was made possible by a gift from Virginia Ullman. Throughout her life, she has cultivated an enduring passion for the oceans and the seashore. Her support of this book is one small grain of sand in a lifetime of effort that has benefited us all.

Copyright © 2002 Biosphere 2 Center

Published by Hartman Publishing Company, Oracle, Arizona.
All rights reserved.
No part of this book may be reproduced in any form or
by any electronic or mechanical means including information storage and
retrieval systems without permission in writing from the publisher,
except by a reviewer who may quote brief passages in a review.

First Edition

Library of Congress Control Number: 2001099503
ISBN 0970349017

Printed in the United States of America
on Recycled Paper

Biosphere 2 Center Mission

Biosphere 2 Center is a nonprofit education and research affiliate of Columbia University, one of eight centers in the Earth Institute at Columbia University. The mission of Biosphere 2 Center is, through excellence and scientific research and education:

- to serve as a center for teaching, learning, and research about Earth and its systems;
- to catalyze interdisciplinary thinking and understanding about Earth and its future;
- to be a key center for Earth education and for outreach to industry, government and the general public;
- to focus public attention on the issues related to Earth systems planning and management.

Grandma Meriweather loved cranberries and seashells and clouds, but most of all she loved stories. "A good story is like a smile," she always said. "A good story can make any situation better."

"Can you tell me a story that will help me get a dog?" her grandson Alex asked one morning. He had begged his parents for a dog for three months but they always said no.

Grandma Meriweather thought about this all day. That evening she told him a story called *The Boy Who Wanted Everything But Never Helped Out.* After hearing that story, Alex began doing his chores. Two months later, he got a dog for his birthday.

When the children in the neighborhood learned how Alex got his dog, they started asking Grandma Meriweather to tell them stories. She would sit on her front porch with her "Magic Bag" and kids would put in words. Then, when the bag was full, she would pull out three words and tell a story.

One day, she pulled out the words: RED CORAL HOUSE

This is the story she told . . .

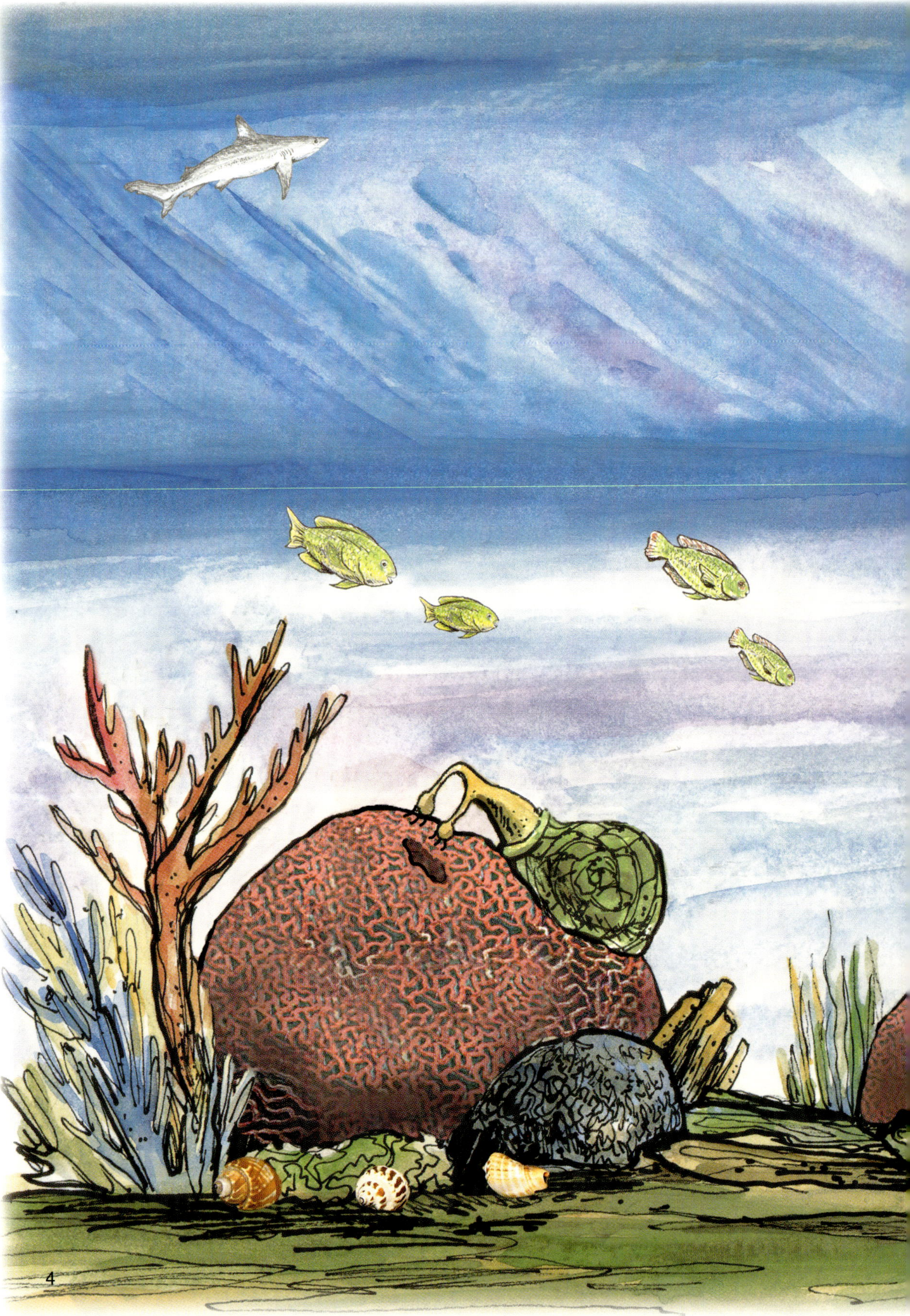

Once upon a time, in a warm ocean far, far away, a sleepity snail named Samantha decided she was all grown up and it was time to leave home. She ate breakfast, said goodbye to her parents and wandered off across the reef.

She hadn't gone very far when suddenly she began to worry. "What will I do?" she wondered out loud. "Where will I spend the night?"

"Excuse me," a small voice said from a peephole in the reef. "Did you say something?"

"Why yes!" Samantha said, peering into the hole. "I'm lost and I'm looking for a place to sleep. Can you help me?"

"I can be your friend," said the little voice. "Having a friend is always helpful. But it seems to me you don't need a place to sleep because your home is on your back."

Samantha thought about this and it made her feel better. "You're right! I can sleep wherever I want."

"You are lucky my friend," said the voice in the hole. "I wish my home was on my back. I've got to stay in this coral colony or I'll get swept away in the current."

"Who are you?"

"My name is Carol and I'm a coral," the voice said, poking her head out. "Actually I'm a polyp but that's a complicated story. Hey, it looks cool out here. I'd love to see the rest of this reef."

Suddenly an idea struck Samantha. "Would you like to go on a walkabout with me? You can join me in my shell."

"Count me in," Carol cried as she zipped out of her coral castle and slipped into Samantha's shell.

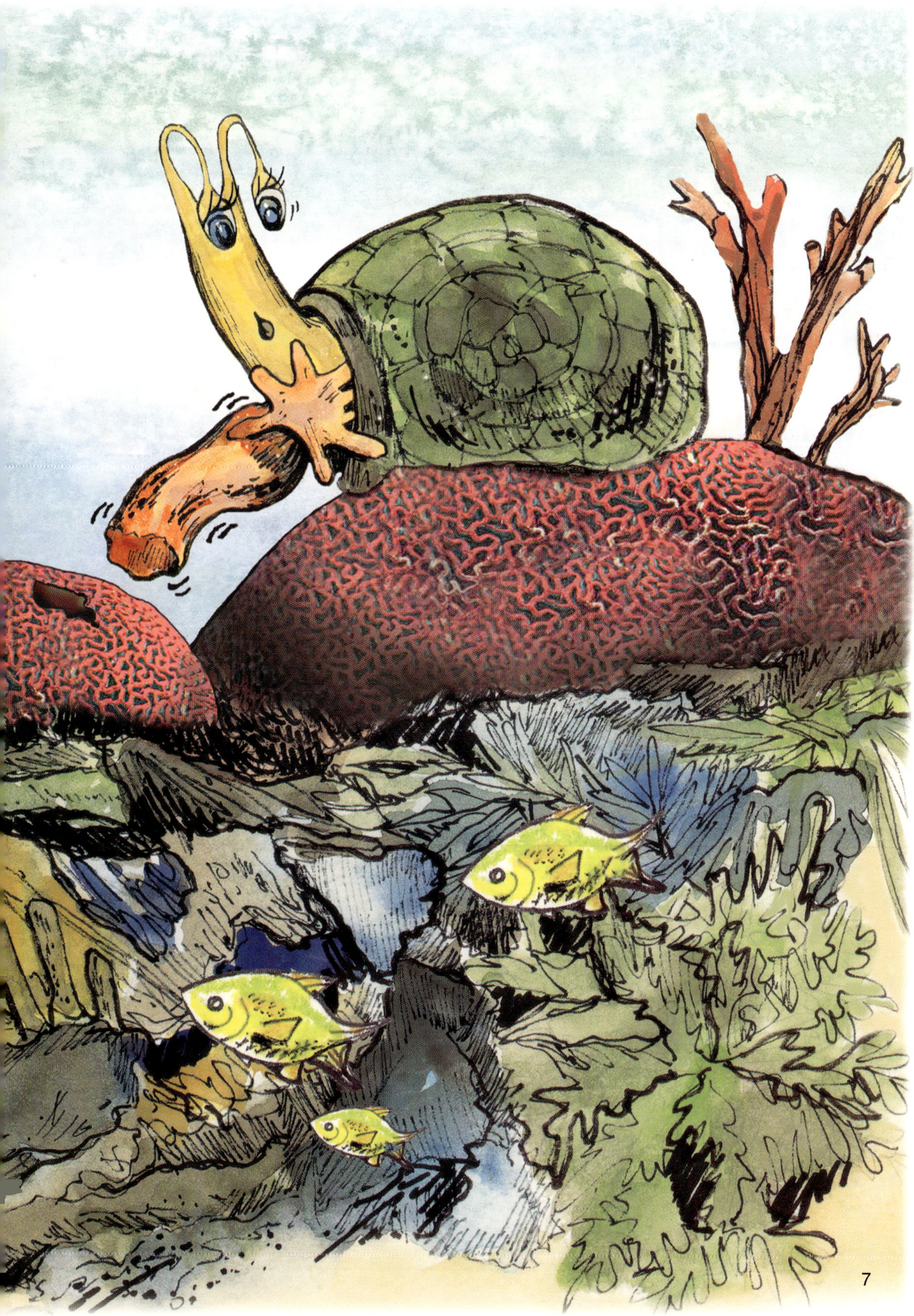

"Cool house," said Carol the coral. "It's safe and roomy in your shell."

Samantha started laughing. "Hey, that tickles. Cut it out! That's my belly you're walking on! Oooo … ahhhh … Now you're on my foot. Stop!"

"Sorry," said Carol. "I didn't realize you were such a tickle baby."

"I'm only ticklish inside my shell," Samantha replied. "Be gentle when you move around in there!"

"Maybe this will work better if I ride on top," Carol said, as she carefully climbed out of Samantha's shell. "By the way, where are we going?"

Samantha yawned. "I don't know . . . but I'm feeling a little bit tired. Maybe we should rest awhile."

"I have an idea! Let's go visit my uncle. He lives in a red coral house on the other side of the reef."

Samantha yawned again. "That sounds great but I'm feeling a little sleepity. I need a rest."

"Wait! You can sleep at my uncle's house. He has a big red bed with lots of pillows."

But it was already too late. Samantha was fast asleep.

Coral Reef Facts

- Coral reefs cover 1/500 of the oceans' area and yet they provide home to 1/3 of all marine fish species.

- Coral reefs are vital to U.S. fisheries. Approximately 1/2 of all federally-managed fisheries depend on coral reefs for part of their life cycle.

- Coral reefs offer great promise for pharmaceuticals now being developed as possible cures for cancer, arthritis, bacterial infections and other diseases.

- About 500 million people depend on coral reefs for food and coastline protection.

For more information, please visit the website of the National Oceanic and Atmospheric Administration (NOAA): www.noaa.gov

When Samantha woke up, the two new friends began their walkabout. Carol kept a lookout for the red coral house while the sleepity snail slunkered over the reef.

Coral reefs are home to millions of plants and animals. It took a long time to reach the other side of the reef because Samantha moved very slowly and stopped several times to admire some of her favorites.

When Samantha and Carol finally reached the other side of the reef, there was no red coral house. All the coral was speckled and spotted white!

"Where's your uncle's house?" Samantha wondered.

"I don't know," said Carol.

Suddenly a strange voice said:
> "I can explain it, if you'll listen to me,
> There are forces at work that are changing the sea."

"Who's talking?" Carol yelled. "Come out where I can see you."

A wise old grouper with floppy glasses swam into view and stopped right in front of Carol and Samantha.

**"Hi! I'm Professor Fish and I'm here to teach,
About life in the ocean and shells on the beach!"**

"Where did you come from?" Samantha asked. "Where is your home?"

**"I live on the reef with all of my friends
And where do I sleep? It all depends,
On the currents, the food and the mood of the sea,
Anywhere on the reef – that's where I'll be!"**

"Enough of that!" cried Carol the coral. "I want to know where my uncle's house is."

**"The coral used to be red but now it's white,
Excess heat gave the plants a fright."**

"Stop the rhymes already. I want you to explain it to me so I can understand. What does heat have to do with my uncle's red coral house?"

Professor Fish cleared his gills and began.

"Once upon a time, in a cooler ocean long, long ago, coral polyps built colorful stony homes. Some polyps like your uncle built red coral castles. But recently, many of these coral reefs have turned white and begun to die."

"Oh no," Carol gasped. "That's no good! Why are coral reefs dying?"

"It's happening because the oceans are getting warmer," Professor Fish replied. "Scientists have recorded higher and higher temperatures in oceans all over the world."

"How does heat kill the coral?" Carol wondered.

"When the ocean gets too hot, a little plant that lives with the coral floats away in the current, looking for a cooler place to live. The coral polyps need this plant for food. This plant also gives the reef its color. So when these plants leave, the red reef turns white and the coral colony begins to die."

Global Climate Change

Evidence that the climate is changing includes the facts that:

- Recent years have been among the warmest this century and the average growing season in northern countries has increased by three weeks.
- The world's glaciers are melting and sea level has risen 6-8 inches in the 20th century.
- CO_2 levels in the atmosphere have risen 30% in the last 100 years and are continuing to rise.

For more information, please visit the NOAA website at: www.noaa.gov

Global Climate Change and Greenhouse Gases

- Human activity has increased the concentration of greenhouse gases in the atmosphere. Greenhouse gases trap heat close to the earth and help raise the surface temperature.
- Most of this increase is carbon dioxide from the combustion of fossil fuels. Carbon dioxide levels have increased by more than 30% since the start of the Industrial Revolution and could double by 2065 if present trends continue.
- Burning one gallon of gas generates 22 pounds of carbon dioxide. When gas is burned, the carbon in it combines with oxygen in the air to form carbon dioxide. Because the oxygen adds weight, the newly formed carbon dioxide weighs more than the original unburned fuel.

For more information, please visit the NOAA website at: www.noaa.gov

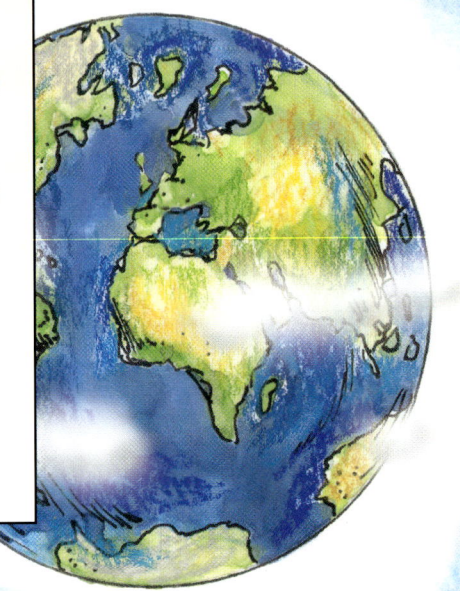

"So, are you telling me coral reefs are dying because the ocean is getting too warm?" Carol asked.

Professor Fish nodded yes.

"Well, what is making the oceans warmer?" Carol wanted to know.

Professor Fish shook his head. **"This is puzzling scientists. Some believe it could be caused by human activity but they just don't know."**

Carol turned to Samantha. "That's a sad story. I didn't know coral reefs were dying."

"Yes, that's a very sad story," Samantha agreed. "In fact, it's so sad it makes me sleepity."

"Wait!" cried Carol, prying open Samantha's eyes. "Hang in there girlfriend!"

But it was too late. Samantha was once again fast asleep.

"This is so frustrating! I wish Samantha could stay awake long enough for us to find my uncle's house. Professor Fish, why is my snail friend so sleepity?"

"There could be many reasons. Maybe the warm water makes her sleepity. Or maybe she sleeps a lot because she's young. Young animals need more sleep than adults you know, because they are growing."

Just then a school of young stripers swam into view. They were playing tag and the orange stripers were `it.' When they saw Professor Fish talking with Carol, they stopped their game and raced over to listen.

"What'd he say? What'd he say? What'd he say?" the young stripers asked, all of them talking at the same time.

Professor Fish smiled as the little stripers gathered in front of him. Then he calmly turned to Carol and said, **"Excuse me. I must give these youngsters a quick lesson before we continue our conversation."**

The lesson was about clam shells. You can tell how old a clam is by counting the growth ridges on its shell, just like with tree rings.

Can you find the youngest desk in the school? Can you find oldest desk in the school?

Global Climate Change and Coral Reefs

- Increased temperatures in the oceans across the world have caused significant coral bleaching.
- An increase in ocean temperature is likely to harm coral reefs and weaken their ability to cope with other problems such as water pollution and storm damage.
- Research at Columbia University's Biosphere 2 shows that climate change will slow reef building by 40% in the middle of the twenty-first century.

For more information, please visit the website of Columbia University's Biosphere 2: www.bio2.columbia.edu

"Where were we?" Professor Fish asked as the stripers sped away, playing another game of tag. This time the purple stripers were `it.'

"You were telling me about how the oceans are getting warmer," Carol answered. "But what I really want to do is find my uncle's house. Can you tell me where it is? All I see around here are empty homes that look like bones."

"It's curious you should mention bones. Coral is light and strong and porous, just like bones. Doctors sometimes use coral to replace injured or diseased bones in people. Doctors also use coral to make medicines."

"That's cool that coral is used to replace bones," Carol said, "but you haven't answered my question. What happened to my uncle's house?"

Professor Fish adjusted his glasses and finally told her the answer. **"It turned white,"** he said. **"It was bleached by the heat. You already passed it on your journey but you didn't recognize it because it was white."**

Carol was alarmed. "Is my uncle still alive?"

"I don't know. You'll have to go back and find out."

"Then that's what we'll do," Carol cried. "We'll leave the minute my sleepity friend wakes up."

Just then Samantha yawned. "Did that strange talking fish with the glasses leave already? He sure seemed smart."

"I'm still here," Professor Fish said, **"but it's time to leave. There's more students out there, I do believe."**

"Good-bye!" cried Carol. "You've taught me a lot. I'll find my uncle before he gets too hot."

Professor Fish smiled. Then he waved his fin and swam away.

"What do you want to do now?" Samantha asked.

Carol immediately answered:
> "We've got to find my uncle's home,
> No matter how far we have to roam.
> He's back on the reef with nothing to eat,
> His red house turned white because of the heat."

Samantha cast a curious eye toward her friend. "There's something strange about the way you're talking," she said. "You're starting to sound like Professor Fish. Maybe we should rest awhile and think about this."

"Oh no," cried Carol. "That will never do! We've got to get going. I'll talk normal if you promise to stay awake!"

Samantha smiled. "I'll try," she said, "but sometimes I get awful sleepity. Maybe I can take a nap when we get to your uncle's house."

"That's a great idea," Carol agreed. "Let's get started."

And so the two friends turned around and headed back across the reef, looking for Carol's uncle. Carol chattered on and on about everything they saw, hoping to keep Samantha awake. "Am I right, girlfriend?" she kept asking. "Isn't this the most beautiful place in the world?"

The sleepity snail just smiled. With her best friend on her back and a good nap in her future, Samantha was as happy as she had ever been.

Every time Grandma Meriweather finished a story, she chose one child to ask a final question. This time a small girl asked, "Did they ever find the uncle's house?"

Grandma Meriweather nodded. "Yes, they did, but it had turned completely white. Carol's uncle was very hungry and sick so they moved him to another part of the reef. They found a place where the water was cooler and the red coral was still alive. And then, finally, Samantha got to sleep in a red coral house."